SCENE BY SCENE COMPARATIVE WORKBOOK HL17

JUNO

by Jason Reitman

Theme/Issue - Relationships

Literary Genre

General Vision and Viewpoint

Copyright © 2016 by Amy Farrell.

All rights reserved. No part of this publication may be reproduced, distributed or transmitted in any form or by any means, including photocopying, recording, or other electronic or mechanical methods, without the prior written permission of the publisher, except in the case of brief quotations embodied in critical reviews and certain other noncommercial uses permitted by copyright law. For permission requests, write to the publisher, addressed "Attention: Permissions Coordinator," at the address below.

Scene by Scene
11 Millfield, Enniskerry
Wicklow, Ireland.
www.scenebysceneguides.com

info@scenebysceneguides.com

Juno Comparative Workbook HL17 by Amy Farrell. —1st ed.
ISBN 978-1-910949-41-2

Juno Comparative Study Workbook

This workbook is designed to help Leaving Certificate English students become familiar with the Comparative Study modes and to understand how each mode may be applied to *Juno*.

The Comparative Study Modes at Higher Level for 2017 are:

Theme/Issue

The theme covered in this workbook is Relationships. This theme can be applied to any relationship in a text and covers love, marriage, friendship and family bonds.

Consider the complexities of relationships and the impact they have on characters' lives.

Literary Genre

This mode refers to the way the story is told.

Consider aspects of narration such as the manner and style of narration, characterisation, setting, tension, literary techniques, etc.

The General Vision and Viewpoint

This mode refers to the author's outlook or view of life and how this viewpoint is represented in the text.

Consider whether the text is bright or dark, optimistic or pessimistic, uplifting or bleak, etc.

How Does it Work?

This workbook has three parts, one each for Theme/Issue (our chosen theme for study is Relationships), Literary Genre and General Vision and Viewpoint. Each part has three sections: Know the Text, Know the Mode and Compare the Texts.

Know The Text

These questions are on *Juno* and refer specifically to this film. Through answering these questions you will get to know the text well, while also getting a feel for the Comparative Study mode the questions relate to.

Know the Mode

These questions use 'mode' specific terms and phrases and are intended to help prepare you for tackling exam questions. They focus on the mode itself, rather than the text you have studied. You apply your knowledge of the text to the mode in question.

Compare the Texts

These questions ask you to compare your texts under specific aspects of each mode. It is important that you get used to the idea of comparing and contrasting your chosen texts, as this is what the Comparative Study is all about. It is good practice to think about your texts in terms of their similarities and differences within each mode.

This approach is designed to prevent 'drift' between modes and focuses on analysis and personal response, rather than summary.

Theme/Issue - Know the Text

1 What are your first impressions of the teenagers' relationship?

2 "I'm sorry I had sex with you. I know it wasn't your idea." - Juno
Whose idea was it?
What does this tell you about their relationship?

| 3 | "She's just...different." - Bleeker's Mom. How does Bleeker's mother's dislike of Juno complicate things? |

| 4 | Why doesn't Bleeker go to the ultrasound with Juno? Does he want to go, in your opinion? |

KNOW THE TEXT

5 Does Bleeker cope well with Juno's pregnancy?
How does this affect their relationship?

6 How does Juno react when she hears Bleeker is going to the prom with Katrina?
What is your reponse to this?

7 "You broke my heart." - Paulie Bleeker.
Did Juno break Bleeker's heart?
Explain your view.

8 Are Juno and Bleeker good **friends**? Explain.
Does this help their relationship?

9 What **strengths** do you see in Juno and Bleeker's relationship?

10 What **weaknesses** or problems do you see in Juno and Bleeker's relationship?

| 11 | What **complicates** their relationship? |

| 12 | Are Juno and Bleeker a good match? |

KNOW THE TEXT

13 How does their relationship **change** and **develop** over the course of the story?

14 Is this a positive or negative relationship?

15 Do Mark and Vanessa have a good relationship? Explain your view.

16 Do Juno and her friend Leah have a good relationship? Explain your view.

KNOW THE TEXT

17 How do her father and stepmother react when she tells them she's pregnant?
What does this tell you about their relationship?

18 Juno tells her father the truth about who the father is. What does this suggest about their relationship?

19 How does Brenda defend Juno at the ultrasound?

20 Why does Brenda discourage Juno from visiting Mark and Vanessa, in your view?

KNOW THE TEXT

21 Does Juno's dad understand her well? Does he love and support her?

22 Does Juno have a good relationship with her father? Explain your view.

JUNO - THEME/ISSUE - RELATIONSHIPS

23 Does Juno have a good relationship with her stepmother, Brenda? Explain your view.

24 Do you think Juno would have coped as well with her pregnancy and the adoption without the support of her family and friends?

Theme/Issue - Know the Mode

25 Are relationships in this text generally **positive** (warm, supportive, nurturing, genuine) or **negative** (cold, cruel, destructive, false)?

26 What makes relationships in this text complicated and **difficult**?

KNOW THE MODE

27 What would **improve** relationships in this text? Give specific examples.

28 How do relationships **change** during the story?

KNOW THE MODE

29 What did **you learn** about relationships from watching this film?

30 Are relationships **portrayed realistically** in this text? Make use of examples to support the points you make.

KNOW THE MODE

31 Are relationships in this story **interesting** and **involving**?

32 Did anything about the theme of relationships in this text **shock, upset** or **unsettle** you?

33 What is the **most signficant relationship** in this text?
What makes it so significant and important?

34 Do relationships in this story bring characters **happiness** or **sorrow**?

KNOW THE MODE

35 Choose **key moments** from this story that highlight relationships in the text.

Theme/Issue - Compare the Texts

36 Were relationships in *Juno* more positive and supportive than the relationships in your other texts? Give specific examples.

37 Rank the relationships you have studied in your various texts from most positive to most negative. Add a note to explain your choices.

38 Were relationships in *Juno* the most engaging and interesting that you have studied?
Explain your choice.

39 Rank the relationships you have studied in your various texts from most interesting to least interesting. Add a note to explain your choices.

40 Did you **learn most** about the theme of relationships from this text or another text on your comparative course?

JUNO - THEME/ISSUE - RELATIONSHIPS

41 What **similarities** do you notice in the theme of relationships in this text and your other comparative texts?

COMPARE THE TEXTS

42 What **differences** do you notice in the theme of relationships in this text and your other comparative texts?

COMPARE THE TEXTS

Literary Genre - Know the Text

43   How is this story told? (Consider the film format).

44   Why is the story told in this way?
What is the effect of this?

KNOW THE TEXT

45 What are your first impressions of Juno?

46 Is she a likeable character?

47 How does Hooper develop Juno's character?

48 What was your initial view of Paulie Bleeker? Did your opinion of him change?

KNOW THE TEXT

49 Is there humour in this story? Explain.

50 How does Juno's first meeting with Mark and Vanessa go? How does this add to the story?

51 Do Juno and Mark get on well? How is this shown? What are you expecting to happen next?

52 What does Juno seeing Vanessa in the mall add to the story?

| 53 | What **obstacles** is Juno met with? Does she overcome these difficulties? |

| 54 | What **music** is used in the soundtrack? How does this contribute to the movie? |

55 Why is the scene where Mark tries to back out of the adoption **dramatic**?

56 Is this a **realistic** story?
Is it an accurate portrayal of an unplanned teenage pregnancy, in your view?

KNOW THE TEXT

57 Are there **fairytale elements** to this story? Explain.

58 Is this story **predictable**?
Did you expect Juno to make the choices she does?

59 In its review, *Empire* called *Juno* "A sharp-edged, sweet-centred, warm-hearted coming-of-age movie that's always just that little bit smarter than you think it is."
Do you agree or disagree with these comments?

Literary Genre - Know the Mode

60 Did **you** enjoy the **storyline** of the text?
Was it exciting/compelling/tense/emotional?
Why/why not?

61 Is there just one **plot** or many plots?
What connections can you make between the storylines?

62 What three things interested **you** most in the story?

63 Are **characters** vivid, realistic and well-developed?

64 Do **you** empathise or **identify** with any character(s)?
Did you become involved in this story or care about the characters? Use examples.

65 Who was your **favourite character**?
What aspects of this character did you enjoy?

66 Consider Juno as the film's **heroine**. What made Juno a **memorable** or **interesting** character?

67 Who was your **least favourite character**? What aspects of this character did you dislike? What made them a memorable or interesting character?

KNOW THE MODE

68 Is the story humorous or tragic, romantic or realistic? Explain using examples.

69 To what **genre** does it belong?
What aspects of this genre did **you** enjoy?
Is it Romance, Thriller, Horror, Action/Adventure, Historical, Fantasy, Science-fiction, Satire, etc.?

70 How does the director create **suspense**, **high emotion** and **excitement** in the text? What **techniques** does he use to good advantage?

71 Consider the director's use of **tension** and **resolution** in the film. What are the major **tensions/problems/conflicts** in the text? Are they **resolved** or not?

JUNO - LITERARY GENRE

72 Did the director make use of any striking patterns of **imagery** or **symbols** to add to the story?

73 How does the director make use of the **unexpected** in this text? What does this add to the story? (Think about key moments here.)

KNOW THE MODE

74 What is the **climax** (high point) of the story?

75 What did **you** think of this moment?
How did it make **you feel**?

| 76 | Comment on the **language** of the film. How does this spoken dimension add to the story? |

| 77 | Comment on the **pacing** of the film. How does this add to the story? |

78 Comment on the **setting** of the film.
Consider time, place, and specific locations such as Juno's school and the abortion clinic. How does setting add to your understanding of the characters and their story?

79 Was anything about this film **moving** or **emotional**?
Think of moments in the film that you responded to. What made them moving? How did this add to the story?

80 On a scale of one to ten, how much did you enjoy the **ending**? What was satisfying/unsatisfying about it? Was anything left unanswered?

81 The experiences of seeing a play, reading a novel and viewing a film are very different.
What aspects of the **film form** worked well in this story, in your opinion?

82 What did **you** like about **the way** the story was told?
*Mention aspects of storytelling and literary techniques that **you** found enjoyable. Refer to key moments.*

83 Identify **key moments** in the film that illustrate Literary Genre (the way the story is told). Clearly **define literary techniques/aspects of narrative** in your analysis.

Literary Genre - Compare the Texts

84 Did **you** like the way this story was told more than your other comparative texts?
State what you enjoyed most about each.

85

Is *Juno* more **exciting** than your other texts?
Consider tension, pacing, suspense, conflict and the unexpected.

86 Are **characters** more engaging in this film than in your other texts?
Refer to each of your texts in you answer.

87 Is the **setting** more effective in telling this story than in your other texts?
Refer to each of your texts in your answer.

88 Is this story more **unpredictable** than your other texts?
Refer to each of your texts in your answer.

89

Did this film have greater **emotional power** than your other texts?
Was emotional power created in a more interesting way here or in a different text?

JUNO - LITERARY GENRE

90 What **similarities** do you notice in the Literary Genre of this film and your other comparative texts?
Mention specific aspects of narrative.

COMPARE THE TEXTS

91 What **differences** do you notice in the Literary Genre of this film and your other comparative texts?
Mention specific aspects of narrative.

COMPARE THE TEXTS

General Vision and Viewpoint - Know the Text

92 Does Juno cope well when she discovers her unplanned pregnancy? How does her **attitude** affect the mood of the film?

93 How does Bleeker react to Juno's pregnancy? Why does he react this way?

KNOW THE TEXT

94 Is her decision to have the baby adopted a positive or negative development?

95 Juno's father and stepmother are very supportive of her pregnancy and decision to have the baby adopted.
How does this add to the film's atmosphere?

96 "No, I don't want to, you know, sell the thing. I just want the baby to be with people who are gonna love it and be good parents, you know?" How does Juno's **outlook** contribute to the General Vision and Viewpoint of the film?

97 What impact has meeting Juno made on Vanessa and Mark's lives?
Is this something positive or negative?

KNOW THE TEXT

98 Is the ultrasound a positive or negative experience for Juno?

99 How do you feel when Juno encourages Bleeker to go out with Katrina de Vort?
Why does she do this?

100 "What, are you ashamed that we did it?" - Juno. Juno is jealous and angry that Bleeker is going to the prom. What is the atmosphere like at this point? How do you feel watching this scene?

101 How does Mark leaving Vanessa affect the **mood** of the story?

KNOW THE TEXT

102 "I need to know that it's possible that two people can stay happy together forever." - Juno.
Is this what this film is about?
Is this a hopeful or hopeless notion?

103 "I think I'm in love with you." - Juno to Bleeker.
How does Juno's statement here affect the film's mood?

> **104** "Someday you'll be back here honey... on your own terms" - Mac MacGuff
> Is the scene in the hospital sad? Explain.

> **105** "He didn't feel like ours. I think he was always hers." How do Juno's words here make you feel? Is the baby lucky to have Vanessa? Explain.

106 Does Juno have a happy ending? Explain your view.

107 What is Jason Reitman telling us about life in this story?
What is Jason Reitman's message?
Is his outlook positive or negative, in your view?

General Vision and Viewpoint - Know the Mode

108 Identify bright/hopeful/optimistic aspects of the film.

109 Identify dark/hopeless/pessimistic aspects of the film.

| 110 | Is this text **optimistic** or **pessimistic**? Explain. *Consider characters' happiness, imagery, atmosphere, future prospects, etc.* |

| 111 | On a scale of one to ten, how optimistic is this text? |

112 Identify the **aspects of life** that the director concentrates on.
Are they positive or negative?
Consider love, understanding, bravery, determination, fear, etc.

113. What **comments** do characters make on their **society** and the problems they're facing?

KNOW THE MODE

114 Are characters happy or unhappy?

115 What makes characters in this story happy and fulfilled?

116 What makes characters in this story unhappy and unfulfilled?

117 Are **relationships** destructive or nurturing? What do they reveal about life, as we see characters supported/thwarted in their efforts to grow/mature?

118 Are **imagery** and **language** bright or dark in the text? (Tone of the text)

JUNO - GENERAL VISION AND VIEWPOINT

119 What is the **mood** of this text?

120 What does this story **teach us about life?**
What do we learn about life's hardships? Are struggles overcome? Is determination rewarded? Is life difficult or joyful?

121 How do you **feel** as you watch this film?
Refer to key moments to anchor your answer.

122 How do you **feel** at the **end**?

123 Are **questions** raised by the text **resolved** by the end?
Are they resolved **happily** or **unhappily**?

124 Are **you hopeful** or **despairing** regarding the prospects for human **happiness** in this story?
Are characters likely to be happy?

125 Identify the **key moments** in the film that illustrate the General Vision and Viewpoint of the text.

KNOW THE MODE

General Vision and Viewpoint - Compare the Texts

126 Is life happier for characters in this story than in your other comparative texts? Explain.

COMPARE THE TEXTS

127 Do characters in this text face more obstacles and difficulties than in your other texts?
Who struggles most?

128 Are characters in this text **rewarded more** for their struggles than in your other texts?
By overcoming adversity, do they achieve true happiness and contentment in a way that is not realised in your other texts?

129 Is this the brightest, most hopeful and triumphant text you have studied? Explain why its message is more or less positive than your other texts.

130 Which of your chosen texts was the bleakest and most upsetting or depressing?
Explain why it was more negative than your other texts. What made them more positive?

131 Plot your three texts on a scale of one to ten, from darkest (most pessimistic) to brightest (most optimistic). Add points to explain their position.

132 What **similarities** do you notice in the General Vision and Viewpoint of this text and your other comparative texts?

COMPARE THE TEXTS

133 What **differences** do you notice in the General Vision and Viewpoint of this text and your other comparative texts?

COMPARE THE TEXTS

www.ingramcontent.com/pod-product-compliance
Lightning Source LLC
Chambersburg PA
CBHW050714090526
44587CB00019B/3372